Hello U.S.A.

OREGON

Gretchen Bratvold

Lerner Publications Company

LIBRARY OF CONGRESS
CATALOGING-IN-PUBLICATION DATA
Bratvold, Gretchen.
    Oregon / Gretchen Bratvold.
        p.   cm. — (Hello USA)
    Includes index.
    Summary: Introduces the geography, history, industries, people, and other highlights of Oregon.
    ISBN 0-8225-2704-9 (lib. bdg.)
    1. Oregon—Juvenile literature.
[1. Oregon.] I. Title. II. Series.
F876.3.B73   1991
979.5—dc20   90-38213
                                     CIP
                                      AC

Cover photograph courtesy of Portland Rose Festival Assoc.

The glossary on page 69 gives definitions of words shown in **bold type** in the text.

Manufactured in the United States of America
1 2 3 4 5 6 7 8 9 10 99 98 97 96 95 94 93 92 91

 This book is printed on recycled paper.

OREGON

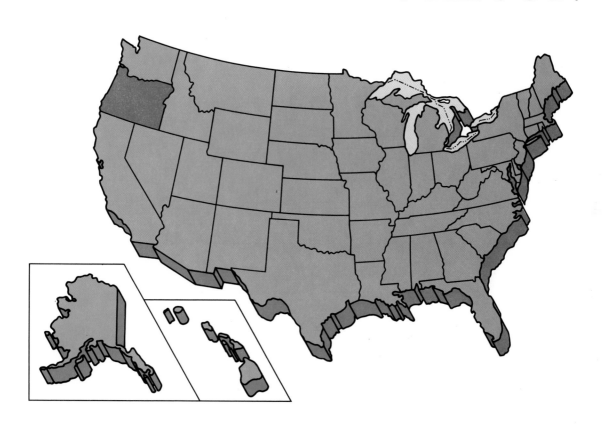

CONTENTS

Did You Know . . . ?

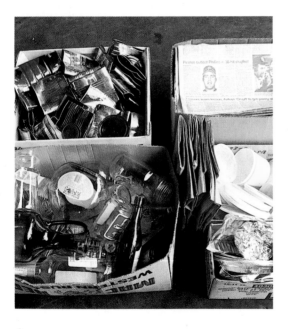

☐ The name *Oregon* may have come from the name French people gave the Columbia River. They called this waterway *Ouragan,* which means "hurricane," probably because of the strong rainstorms that blow in from the sea and travel up the river.

☐ Some of the fir trees in Oregon's forests are over 1,000 years old. They can measure over 250 feet (76 meters) tall—that's almost as high as the Statue of Liberty!

☐ In 1971 Oregon became the first state to require that all beverage cans and bottles be returnable.

☐ Western Oregon gets so much rain that the people who live there have been nicknamed Webfoots. Folklore says that babies in the region are born with webs between their toes so they can paddle, like ducks, across wet land.

☐ The Oregon Trail was the longest overland route traveled by pioneers moving west. Starting in Missouri and ending in Oregon's Willamette Valley, the trail stretched across 2,000 miles (3,220 km) of prairie, mountains, and desert. The difficult journey took four to six months by covered wagon.

Saddle Mountain, one of the highest peaks in the Coast Ranges, offers a good view of the surrounding area.

n ranges cover most of The Coast Ranges ng the western strip of ese mountains are the e state. Along much of teep cliffs rise sharply an. Inland, the north-he Coast Ranges flat-o the valley of the Willamette River. This small but fertile area is home to more than half of Oregon's people.

East of the Coast Ranges, the Cascade Mountains divide western Oregon from eastern Oregon. The highest mountains in the state, the Cascades contain several peaks that rise over 10,000 feet (3,048 m).

A Trip Around the State

Sometimes called the Pacific Wonderland, Oregon is located on the Pacific coast of the northwestern United States. Mountains, sand dunes, and misty shores make the state an out-door paradise. Washington, Idaho, Nevada, and California border the state on three sides, and the Pacific Ocean washes against Oregon's western shore.

9

Millions of years ago, shallow seas covered part of what is now Oregon and the land was much flatter. Gradually, the seas dried up and the earth's crust began to shift, pushing up mountains along the western coast. Deep underground, gases and molten rock began to bubble up to the earth's surface, and volcanoes erupted. They spouted ash and **lava,** melted rock that hardens into solid rock as it cools.

Over time, the lava and ash built up higher and higher around the mouths of the volcanoes, eventually forming the Cascade Mountains. Lava also gushed from cracks in the earth's crust and flowed across broad expanses, hardening into layers of rock that is now thousands of feet thick. Oregon's Columbia Plateau, a highland region, was formed this way.

At Lava Lands in central Oregon, visitors can explore a moonlike landscape shaped by volcanoes.

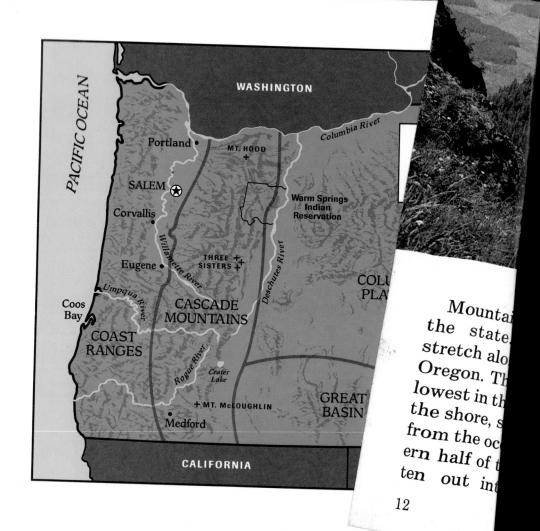

Many of the mountains in
the Cascades—including
Mount Hood—are
volcanoes, but they have
not erupted for centuries.

Walls of sheer rock challenge climbers at Smith Rock State Park on the Columbia Plateau.

The Columbia Plateau fills most of eastern Oregon. Although **plateaus** are usually flat highlands, mountains cover much of this region, especially in the northeast. Streams have cut deep **canyons** into the thick volcanic rock that forms the plateau. Most of the people who live here grow wheat, Oregon's most valuable crop.

South of the Columbia Plateau is a region called the Great Basin. Mountains and valleys extend across this region. Some of the Great Basin is so dry that it is considered **desert**. That means that less than 10 inches (25 centimeters) of rain fall per year. Water from the region's few streams dries up before it can flow out to the ocean.

Rich colors highlight desert areas of the Great Basin in the fall.

15

Hundreds of rivers and streams drain rain and snow from Oregon's Cascade and Coast mountains. The Columbia River, Oregon's biggest, is 7 miles (11 km) wide where it enters the Pacific Ocean. Large, oceangoing ships can travel 200 miles (322 km) up the waterway before it becomes too shallow. The Willamette, Deschutes, and Snake rivers flow into the Columbia.

The Columbia and the Snake rivers have carved deep canyons through the Columbia Plateau. Hells Canyon, along the Snake River, averages a depth of 5,500 feet (1,680 m). Several other rivers—including the Rogue and Umpqua—flow from the Cascades into the Pacific.

Many small lakes dot the slopes of the Cascade Mountains. Crater Lake, the deepest lake in the United States, sits within the collapsed walls of Mount Mazama, an extinct volcano.

Oregon has two different climates—one west of the Cascade Mountains, and another east of this barrier. To the west, temperatures change little throughout the year. This area receives a lot of rain—sometimes over 130 inches (330 cm) in a year.

The ice-cold waters of Crater Lake descend to a depth of 1,932 feet (589 m).

The colorful petals of the Indian paintbrush brighten Oregon's countryside.

When rain clouds move in from the ocean, they must rise to pass over the mountains. As the clouds rise, they drop their moisture on the Coast Ranges and the western slopes of the Cascades. By the time the clouds cross the Cascades, they have lost almost all of their moisture, making the eastern side of the state very dry. Here, temperatures dip below freezing in the winter and average 72° F (22° C) in the summer.

Forests of cedars, firs, pines, ashes, and maples cover western Oregon. But only a few hardy trees can survive in the dry climate east of the Cascades. Grasses and sage-brush are the main plants that are native to this eastern region.

Oregon's wildlife also varies from one side of the Cascades to the other. Elk and deer feed on the lush vegetation of western Oregon. In the east, bighorn sheep and pronghorn antelope climb the rocky slopes. The state is famous for its salmon, which swim from the ocean up Oregon's rivers each spring to lay their eggs. Seals and sea lions feast on fish and squid along the coast.

The pronghorn antelope feeds on the grasses and shrubs of eastern Oregon.

19

Oregon's Story

The first humans in the region now known as Oregon arrived more than 12,000 years ago. These people were American Indians. They lived at a place called Fort Rock Caves. Signs of human life at Fort Rock vanished after 5000 B.C., when Mount Mazama erupted. But **archaeologists** have uncovered some clues to this distant past. Among their finds are stone tools and sandals made from sagebrush bark.

Other Indians lived along the Columbia River, where they caught and dried enough salmon each spring to last the whole year. The people held a huge thanksgiving ceremony to celebrate the first catch of the year. At this feast, they sampled the fish and returned its skeleton to the river.

Little else is known about American Indian life in what is now Oregon before the 1700s, when European explorers arrived in the region. From the explorers we know that several bands of Indians lived in the area at that time. Most of them lived along the coast, where the ocean and thick forests offered plenty of fish and game for food.

The lush forests of western Oregon *(right)* **provided abundant wildlife for Indian hunters. Salmon** *(facing page)* **was a staple in their diet.**

Coastal Indians such as the Chinook and the Tillamook were experienced traders, often using seashells for money. Sometimes they traded with Indians from the Cascade Mountains and the Columbia Plateau.

Native Americans from these eastern regions included the Modoc, Klamath, Nez Percé, and Cayuse. Because most of the area was dry, these Indians lived in villages along rivers. In the spring they caught salmon, and they also dug wild roots for food. During the

Chinook Indians considered flattened foreheads a sign of beauty. To achieve this look, mothers strapped their infants in a cradleboard. This device had a hinged board that was clamped down to shape the head into a straight line from the crown to the tip of the nose.

Indians along the Columbia River wove grass mats to cover a frame of wooden poles. Called longhouses, these portable dwellings could house several people.

1700s, the Nez Percé and Cayuse became skilled horse riders and breeders.

Few Indians lived in the dry Great Basin region to the south, where food was scarce. Those who did live in the area spent much of their time looking for food—nuts, berries, roots, snakes, lizards, insects. Finding enough water and firewood was also a constant challenge. The Paiute and other Indians in this region wove beautiful baskets from grasses that grew there.

Fur traders made huge profits selling furs from sea otters, whose thick fur traps air and keeps out cold and water. By the late 1800s, hardly any of the animals were left.

The first Europeans to stumble upon Oregon's Indians probably came from Great Britain. The British took an interest in the Pacific Northwest in the late 1700s. The explorers James Cook and George Vancouver both thought the region would be ideal for fur trading.

Cook befriended the Chinook. Expert trappers and traders, these Indians exchanged furs from seals and sea otters for knives, nails, buttons, and blankets. Cook's crew discovered they could make a fortune selling the valuable furs. In Asia, where furs were very popular, the animal skins sold for as much as $100 each.

Word of the profits to be made selling furs from the Pacific North-

**Robert Gray's discovery of the Columbia
River strengthened U.S. claim to the region.**

west spread to others. Americans from the newly formed United States (on the eastern side of the continent) also took an interest in the region.

In 1792 Robert Gray, an American, sailed along the coast of the Pacific Northwest. Here, he found a thunderous river and named it after his ship, the *Columbia.*

In 1805 two other American adventurers, Meriwether Lewis and William Clark, reached Oregon the hard way—by land. Lewis and Clark had explored western North America in search of the best land route across the continent to the Pacific Ocean.

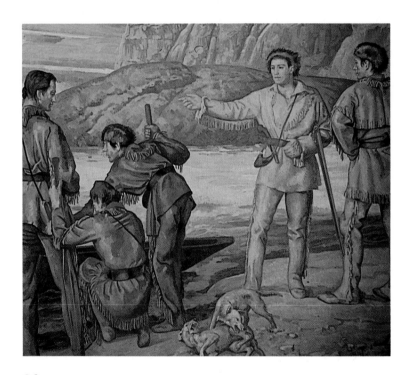

After nearly 18 months of travel, Lewis and Clark finally reached the Columbia River *(left),* which they followed to the Pacific Ocean. This last leg of their journey later became part of the Oregon Trail *(right).* Their entire route is called the Lewis and Clark expedition.

They had traveled 2,000 miles (3220 km)—all the way from Missouri—forging part of the route that became known as the Oregon Trail. At the entrance to the Columbia River, members of the expedition built their winter quarters, which they called Fort Clatsop.

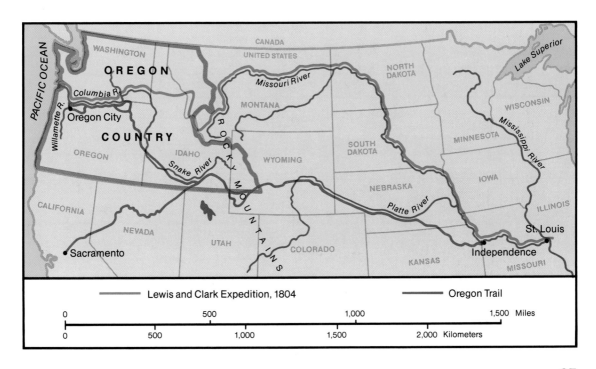

Lewis and Clark Expedition, 1804   Oregon Trail

| 0 | 500 | 1,000 | 1,500 | Miles |
| 0 | 500 | 1,000 | 1,500 | 2,000 | Kilometers |

Both Britain and the United States claimed the Oregon Country—a huge area between California and Alaska and between the Pacific Ocean and the Rocky Mountains. In the early 1800s, both British and American pioneers began to settle in the region.

In 1821 the British asked a man named John McLoughlin to start a fur-trading operation in the Pacific Northwest for the Hudson's Bay Company. In 1825 McLoughlin opened Fort Vancouver (in the present-day state of Washington) near the mouth of the Willamette River.

McLoughlin gave plots of land to people who had worked for the Hudson's Bay Company—an action that encouraged more British people to settle in the region. At the same time, American **missionaries** (Christians who wanted to spread their religion among the Indians) slowly began to arrive in the Pacific Northwest.

Other Americans began to hear stories about Oregon's rich soil. In 1843 about 1,000 people arrived in the first wagon train to travel the Oregon Trail. Most of these **immigrants** (newcomers) chose to farm the fertile Willamette Valley.

At a camp along the Oregon Trail, immigrants pause to eat, rest, and play.

Within two years of the arrival of the first wagon train, Oregon City had grown into a thriving town.

As more Americans settled in the Willamette Valley, Britain and the United States agreed to split the Oregon Country between them. In 1846 the United States took the southern part, where most of the Americans were living, and Britain took the northern portion, in what is now Canada. By 1859, Americans in Oregon had set up a government, and Oregon became the 33rd state to join the Union.

Immigrants continued to come to Oregon, and the Indians in the area began to distrust the white settlers. Wagon trains scared away game, and the newcomers settled on Indian territory. Thousands of Indians died from diseases brought into the region by the immigrants. Indian attacks became common as more settlers arrived.

The U.S. government forced Indian chiefs to sign **treaties**. By signing these agreements, the Native Americans gave up claims to much of their territory. In exchange, the United States gave the Indians a piece of land on which they were told they could live un-disturbed. This land was to be their **reservation**.

Often, the U.S. government did not live up to the terms of the treaties, and it became difficult for the Indians to follow their own way of life. Different tribes were placed on the same reservation. Sometimes the tribes that were put together had been longtime enemies.

Oregon's Indians had traditionally hunted and gathered their food. But on the reservations, government agents forced them to farm crops. The government broke many of its promises to provide education, supplies, and money to the Indians.

Chief Joseph

The Nez Percé War

The Nez Percé at one time proudly claimed that they had never killed a white person. But in the 1860s, gold brought eager white settlers to the Nez Percé reservation. The U.S. government told those Nez Percé who lived in the Wallowa Valley in northeastern Oregon to move to another reservation in Idaho. Some Indians refused to leave.

More white settlers came in 1873, this time to herd cattle. Chief Joseph, leader of the Wallowa band of Nez Percé, did not want to fight, but he also wanted to stay on the land where his parents were buried. He remembered the words of his dying father: "Never sell the bones of your father and your mother."

In 1877 a group of young Nez Percé warriors killed several white people. The whites wanted revenge, and Joseph's people had no choice left but to fight. Joseph had only 200 warriors and another 400 women, children, and old people. The settlers had an entire army—hundreds of soldiers ready to defeat the Nez Percé. Yet, battle after battle, the Nez Percé crushed the heavily armed U.S. troops.

But Joseph knew his people could not win every fight and that their only hope was to escape. For four months they traveled over deserts and mountains, heading toward Canada, where the army would not follow them. The trek was difficult, and food and other supplies frequently ran low. As winter approached, the Indians grew very weary.

Just 30 miles (48 km) from the Canadian border, the U.S. Army caught up to the Nez Percé and surrounded their camp. Chief Joseph knew the end had come. He got on his horse and slowly rode up to the U.S. general.

"I am tired of fighting," Joseph said. "Our chiefs are killed. . . . It is cold and we have no blankets, no food. The little children are freezing to death. . . . My heart is sick and sad. From where the sun now stands, I will fight no more forever."

After a 1,700-mile (2737-km) journey, Joseph's surrender speech captured the feelings of all his people. The leader of the Nez Percé was never permitted to return to his homeland. When Joseph died in 1904, his doctor reported that he had died of a broken heart.

Portland quickly passed Oregon City as the largest community in the Pacific Northwest. By 1888 Portland's population had reached 60,000.

Between 1860 and 1890, thousands of people moved to Oregon from the midwestern United States and from northern Europe. As farmland in the Willamette Valley filled up, immigrants tried their luck at mining or farming on the Columbia Plateau.

Other newcomers chopped down trees or worked at factories in Portland, which had grown to be Oregon's largest city. When the

34

Northern Pacific Railroad opened in 1883, Oregonians began sending lumber and other goods to the eastern coast of the United States at record speeds.

Asians came from China and Japan to work on the railroads or in the mines. They were so eager to get jobs that they worked for very low wages. Many Oregonians disliked the Asians simply because they were different. Some Oregonians kept Asians from voting or owning land.

As railroads were built in Oregon, factories could ship more products to the East Coast.

Oregon's laws were not kind to everyone. But compared to other states Oregon was considered a leader in setting up a fair system of government. The state passed laws that allowed most of its people to participate more directly in the government. They had more control over what became law, and they could vote people out of office.

During the 1930s, Oregonians built Bonneville Dam on the Columbia River. The water that surged through the dam turned huge engines that created electricity. This form of energy—called **hydropower**—provided inexpensive electrical power needed to run machines at many factories. The dam also controlled the level of the

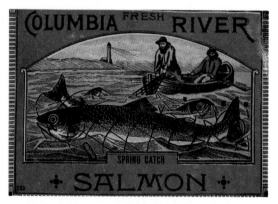

Among the first goods manufactured in Oregon were canned salmon. But by the early 1900s, fewer fish were left to catch and the industry began to decline.

river's water, which made it easier for ships to travel.

More dams were built in the 1950s and 1960s. With the growth of hydropower, more industries came to Oregon to take advantage of the cheap source of energy. In the fields, farmers started using more efficient machinery for some of their chores, so they didn't need as many helping hands. The extra people moved from the country to cities, where they took up work in factories.

Wheat, Oregon's most important crop, thrives in the dry, eastern part of the state. The rise of irrigation in the mid-1900s has allowed farmers to grow more crops.

The new dams provided water for **irrigation** as well as energy for electricity. By irrigating, farmers could channel water from the rivers to their fields. Even areas that did not get much rain could now get enough water for farming. As machinery and irrigation on farms increased, so did the size of harvests. Many crops were sent to be canned at food processing plants in the cities.

During this period, lumbering also flourished, growing into a major business. The state's thick forests provided millions of trees—enough to construct more than half of the new homes built in the United States each year. Until the 1960s, sawdust, bark, and other lumber scraps were thrown away. Then factories began to use these materials to make wood products such as plywood and particle board.

Since the 1970s, forest workers have planted seedlings to replace some of the trees that are cut down each year.

39

| 10,000 B.C. | A.D. 1792 | 1805 | 1821 | 1843 | 1859 | 1877 |

Indians live at Fort Rock Caves in Oregon

Robert Gray is the first white person to sail into the Columbia River

Lewis and Clark expedition reaches Oregon

John McLoughlin comes to Oregon to head the Hudson's Bay Company

First large group of immigrants comes to Oregon in covered wagons

Oregon joins the Union as the 33rd state

Nez Percé War

While the lumber industry was growing, some people wanted to protect Oregon's forests from over-cutting. New trees could not be planted fast enough to replace all the cut trees, and one of Oregon's greatest sources of natural beauty was shrinking.

The conflict between people who want to protect the forests and people who work in the lumber industry continues. More and more Oregonians, however, are beginning to recognize that their forests could disappear if they do not slow down the rate of log cutting.

Bonneville Dam is completed; large ships can now travel 200 miles (322 km) up the Columbia River

Forest Practices Act is enacted to help preserve Oregon's wilderness areas

Oregon's state flag was adopted in 1925. The shield in the center is surrounded by 33 stars, which indicate that Oregon was the 33rd state to join the Union.

Portland is Oregon's largest city.

Living and Working in Oregon

Almost all of Oregon's 2.7 million people were born in the United States. Some Oregonians come from families of European descent who followed the Oregon Trail and settled in Oregon during the 1800s. Others trace their roots to Africa, Asia, or Mexico.

Only 1 percent of the population is Native American. Some Indians live on one of Oregon's four reservations. The largest Indian reservation is Warm Springs, on the eastern side of the Cascade Mountains.

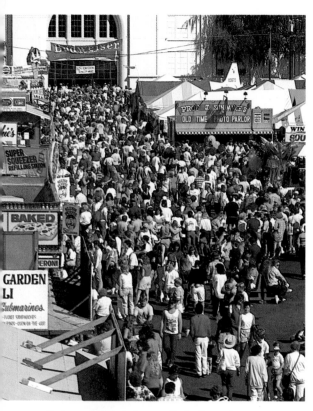

Salem, Oregon's capital city, attracts thousands of people to the State Fair each summer.

Oregon is the 10th largest state in the country, but it ranks 29th in number of people. Even in the state's cities, overcrowding is not a problem. Like the early settlers, most people live in the Willamette Valley, where the largest cities are located. These urban centers include Portland, Eugene, Salem (the capital), and Corvallis. Medford, in the southwest, is the largest city outside the valley.

Much of Oregon's cultural life takes place in Portland, the state's largest city. Portland has its own symphony orchestra and opera company. The Portland Art Museum, the Oregon Museum of Science and Industry, and the Oregon Historical Society draw thousands of visitors each year.

Portland, the City of Roses, hosts the Rose Festival in early June. For the festival's Grand Floral Parade, Portlanders build all-floral floats *(left)*. Several races, including the Dragon Boat Race *(below)*, are also part of the 17-day event.

Some towns feature historical sites or American Indian art museums. Pioneer Village in Jacksonville captures life as it was during a gold rush in the 1850s. Several towns have annual events that celebrate life or history in their community.

45

Among the numerous events held throughout Oregon each year are the Sandcastle Contest in the coastal town of Cannon Beach *(above)*; the Pendleton Round-Up, a rodeo in northeastern Oregon *(upper right)*; and the Mayor's Cup bicycle race in Portland *(right)*.

46

Sports lovers find many exciting possibilities in Oregon. Hunters, fishers, skiers, boaters, hikers, and mountain climbers all enjoy the state's wilderness. Many top runners live in Eugene, the Track Capital of the World, because of its excellent running facilities. The Portland Trail Blazers, a professional basketball team, began competing in 1970.

Like the early settlers, many Oregonians still depend on natural resources such as trees and fertile soil for their livelihood. But compared to the early 1900s, only a few people are still loggers or farmers. More workers now make or sell products that are made from lumber or food crops.

Forests cover almost half of the state, and Oregon is one of the top producers of lumber in the country. Some people in the lumber industry cut timber, plant trees, or make plywood, furniture, or mobile homes. Others work in sawmills or paper mills. Oregon earns more money from making wood products than from any other industry. Many of these items are shipped from Coos Bay, a busy coastal port, to places throughout the world.

Some Oregonians still farm the fertile soil
of the western valleys *(above)*, but more
people work in manufacturing and trade.
Many of the state's products are shipped
overseas from coastal ports *(right)*.

49

In recent years, however, Oregon has made less money from forest products because the demand for these goods has dropped. Many people have lost their jobs. Finding new jobs for all the people who once worked in Oregon's lumber industry is a big challenge.

Gradually the state is building new factories that make high-tech products, such as computers and electrical equipment. Some workers have taken jobs in this field of high technology, Oregon's fastest growing industry. Most of these people live and work just west of Portland, in an area nicknamed Silicon Forest—named after the material (silicon) used to make the small chips that store information in a computer.

Some factories in Oregon freeze, can, or freeze-dry food crops and then sell them to grocery stores throughout the country. Oregonians who work in food processing

Computers are one of several high-tech products made in Oregon.

prepare many types of food for sale, including fruits, vegetables, meat, seafood, cheese, and sugar.

Mild temperatures and plentiful rainfall make western Oregon a good place to grow a wide variety of crops. In the fertile valleys of the west, pears, apples, grapes, cherries, peaches, strawberries, beans, peas, and nuts thrive. Oregon grows more hazelnuts and Christmas trees than any other state in the country.

Oregon's agricultural crops include grapes and apples, which are grown in the west. In the east, beef cattle are a major product.

Some farmers west of the Cascades raise poultry, hogs, and dairy cows, but larger herds of sheep and beef cattle roam the ranches of eastern Oregon. In this dry portion of the state, grains grow well. Wheat, for example, is the state's most valuable crop. Other grains raised in eastern Oregon include hay, barley, and oats. One of the few vegetables planted in the east is the potato.

53

Oregon's rocky beaches, sand dunes, rugged mountains, clear lakes and rivers, and beautiful forests attract many visitors each year. In addition to its natural beauty, Oregon provides many kinds of entertainment in its larger cities. Oregonians who work in hotels, restaurants, and airports provide services to make travelers more comfortable.

Many other service jobs also exist in Oregon. Doctors, teachers, bankers, and shopkeepers have jobs that help others. Those who work for the government also fill service positions. The Forest Service, one of Oregon's largest government agencies, oversees the lumber industry and works to preserve Oregon's wilderness.

At the John Day Fossil Beds in northeastern Oregon, visitors can find signs of prehistoric life—saber-toothed tigers, giant pigs, and three-toed horses.

Protecting the Environment

Oregon has some of the largest forests in the United States. But the rise of logging and other industries since the mid-1800s has threatened the future of Oregon's many trees.

In a state that depends on the lumber industry for money and jobs, protecting the forests is not easy. Some people in the state care most about keeping their present jobs in lumbering. Others care more about preserving Oregon's forests. Still others are concerned about both the forests and the lumber industry.

The government of Oregon has made many laws to protect forests in the state. The Forest Practices Act of 1971 outlines a program to prevent damage to woodlands, streams, and wildlife. The State Department of Forestry teaches loggers to cut trees and build roads in ways that will do less harm to the environment.

These efforts have slowed the destruction of Oregon's forests, but more could be done. Some Oregonians are asking the state's industries and residents to take further steps to protect their environment. These people, called environmentalists, would like to end the logging practice of **clear-cutting** (felling all the trees in an area). Total clearing wipes out the habitats of animals who live in the area.

With no trees left in clear-cut areas, certain kinds of fungi that grow around the roots of many trees die. These small life-forms use the live trees for their source of energy. In turn, the fungi help the trees absorb water and nutrients. Without the fungi, trees planted in clear-cut areas may not survive. Loggers are beginning to thin forests, selecting only some trees for cutting rather than completely clearing an area.

To replace trees that have been felled, the Department of Forestry plants millions of seedlings each year. But it takes 60 to 80 years for the trees to mature. Only a small number of the forests left in Oregon contain old growth—that is, trees that are between 200 and 1,200 years old.

After stripping entire hillsides bare *(below)*, forest workers plant seedlings *(left)*. But the young trees grow too slowly to completely repair the damage caused by clear-cutting.

Spotted Owl

As the old-growth forests disappear, so do some kinds of wildlife that depend on them for habitats. For example, the spotted owl can live only in the thick, dark, older forests. Some environmentalists say spotted owls are in danger of becoming extinct, or dying out entirely.

Because of concern for the spotted owl, for other animals, and for plants, the Department of Forestry has begun to limit the number of trees that can be cut in some areas. As old policies begin to change, the future of Oregon's forests looks brighter.

If Oregon's forests are managed carefully, we can all continue to enjoy the beauty of these woodlands.

61

Oregon's Famous People

Carl Barks (born 1901) is a cartoonist originally from Merrill, Oregon. Barks illustrated the Walt Disney cartoon "Donald Duck" and in 1947 created the character Uncle Scrooge McDuck to add to the comic.

John B. Yeon (born 1910), who is from Portland, taught himself much of what he knows about architecture (designing buildings). He is especially noted for using landscape to make his buildings more attractive.

► JOHN YEON

AHMAD ►
RASHAD

ATHLETES

Ahmad Rashad (born 1949), who originally came from Portland, played professional football from 1972 to 1982. He has also been a sportscaster for NBC Sports.

Alberto Salazar (born 1958) is a runner from Cuba who lives in Eugene, Oregon. He has won the New York City Marathon three times and the Boston Marathon once.

Mary Decker Slaney (born 1958) is a professional runner who lives in Eugene, Oregon. She has set five American and world track records and competed in the 1984 and 1988 Olympics.

◄ JOHN
JACOB
ASTOR

BUSINESS LEADERS & EDUCATORS

John Jacob Astor (1763–1848) was a fur trader who set up the Pacific Fur Company in 1810 to compete with the British fur

◀ DAVID HEIL

PHILIP ▶
KNIGHT

trade in the Oregon Country. The following year, Astor founded the town of Astoria, the first permanent settlement in Oregon.

David R. Heil (born 1955) spent his early years exploring the meadows, woods, and stream in his hometown of Dallas, Oregon. His fascination with nature led him to a career in science education. Since 1988, television viewers across the country have watched him as the host of "Newton's Apple," a Public Broadcasting Service (PBS) science program. Heil is also the associate director of the Oregon Museum of Science and Industry in Portland.

Philip H. Knight (born 1938), a native of Portland, was one of two businessmen who founded Nike, Inc., a sports-gear company named after the Greek goddess of victory. At first called Blue Ribbon Sports, Nike got its start in 1964, when Knight began selling running shoes from his father's basement. By 1990 the company was selling more than one billion dollars worth of sports shoes and other equipment.

EXPLORERS

David Douglas (1798–1834) was a Scottish explorer and botanist. He traveled through California, Oregon, and British Columbia and described the plants he found. The Douglas fir, Oregon's state tree, is named after him.

Robert Gray (1755–1806), a fur trader and explorer, was the first American to sail around the world. Gray discovered and sailed into the Columbia River in 1792. His trip gave the United States a claim to Oregon.

▲ ROBERT GRAY

DAVID DOUGLAS ▶

63

John McLoughlin (1784–1857) was a Canadian who became known as the Father of Oregon. As a fur trader, McLoughlin headed the Hudson's Bay Company and helped build Fort Vancouver in 1825. He encouraged many people to settle in the Oregon Country.

◀ JOHN McLOUGHLIN

MUSICIANS

Tim Hardin (1940–1980), born in Eugene, was a singer and songwriter. He wrote "If I Were a Carpenter," which was recorded by Bobby Darin, Bob Seger, and other singers.

Carl ("Doc") Severinsen (born 1927) is a musician and band leader from Arlington, Oregon. He joined the "Tonight Show" orchestra in 1962 and has been its music director since 1967.

DOC ▶
SEVERINSEN

▲ ABIGAIL
DUNIWAY
(center)

KEINTPOOS ▶

POLITICIANS & LEADERS

Abigail Jane Scott Duniway (1834–1915) was one of the first women in the United States to fight for women's rights. After her husband became an invalid, she supported him and her family of six children by running a hat shop in Albany, Oregon. Her work made her aware of laws that treated men and women unequally, and she began to demand fair treatment for women. Her efforts helped women gain the right to vote in three states—Oregon, Washington, and Idaho.

Keintpoos (died 1873), known as "Captain Jack," led a group of Modoc Indians during the 1860s. Together they fought to maintain their traditional way of life rather than live on a reservation. The U.S. Army eventually captured Keintpoos, and he was tried, found guilty, and executed on October 3, 1873.

Thomas Lawson McCall (1913–1983) served as governor of Oregon from 1967 to 1975. He supported environmental laws, cleaned up Oregon's rivers, and limited building along the coast of Oregon. During McCall's term in office, Oregon passed the first state law in the country requiring beverage cans and bottles to be returnable.

Marcus Whitman (1802–1847), was a physician, pioneer, and missionary. In 1843 he helped guide the first large party of settlers to the Oregon Country. A band of Cayuse Indians massacred him, his wife Narcissa, and 12 others in 1847.

BEVERLY ► CLEARY

 WRITERS & SCIENTISTS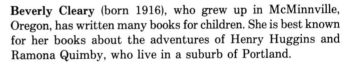

Beverly Cleary (born 1916), who grew up in McMinnville, Oregon, has written many books for children. She is best known for her books about the adventures of Henry Huggins and Ramona Quimby, who live in a suburb of Portland.

Evelyn Sibley Lampman (1907–1980) was born in Dallas, Oregon, and died in Portland. She wrote several books for children, including *The City Under the Back Steps*, *Halfbreed*, and *Cayuse Coyote*. She used the pen name Lynn Bronson on some of her books.

Linus Carl Pauling (born 1901) is a chemist and physicist from Portland. In 1954 he won a Nobel Prize in chemistry for discoveries that helped doctors solve medical problems. Eight years later—in 1962—he won a Nobel Peace Prize for the work he had done to stop the testing of nuclear weapons. Such testing posed a serious health threat to millions of people throughout the world.

▲ LINUS PAULING

Facts-at-a-Glance

Nickname: Beaver State
Song: "Oregon, My Oregon"
Motto: The Union
Flower: Oregon grape
Tree: Douglas fir
Bird: western meadowlark

Population: 2,766,000 (1990 estimate)
Rank in population, nationwide: 29th
Area: 97,100 sq mi (251,489 sq km)
Rank in area, nationwide: 10th
Date and ranking of statehood:
    February 14, 1859, the 33rd state
Capital: Salem
Major cities (and populations*):
    Portland (387,870), Eugene (105,410), Salem
    (93,920), Medford (43,580), Corvallis (39,880),
    Springfield (38,400)
U.S. senators: 2
U.S. representatives: 5
Electoral votes: 7

Places to visit: Bonneville Dam on the Columbia River, Sea Lion Caves near Florence, Crater Lake National Park, Columbia River Gorge, John Day Fossil Beds National Monument

Annual events: Pioneer Day in Jacksonville (June), Portland Rose Festival (June), World Championship Timber Carnival in Albany (July), Pendleton Round-up and Happy Canyon Pageant (Sept.), Kraut and Sausage Feed and Bazaar in Verboort (Nov.)

* 1986 estimates

Average January temperature: 32° F (0° C)	Average July temperature: 66° F (19° C)

Natural resources: timber, limestone, sand, gravel, nickel, natural gas, pumice, coal, clay, copper, gemstones, gold, lead, silver, talc, water, soil

Agricultural products: timber, beef cattle, wheat, milk, potatoes, Christmas trees, grass seed, hazelnuts, fruits

Manufactured goods: lumber and wood products, food products, paper products, metal products, nonelectrical machinery, transportation equipment

ENDANGERED SPECIES
Mammals—Columbia white-tailed deer, gray wolf, humpback whale, blue whale, sperm whale, gray whale
Birds—short-tailed albatross, California least tern, Aleutian Canada Goose, brown pelican
Reptiles—green sea turtle, leatherback sea turtle
Fish—Borax Lake chub, Foskett Spring speckled dace, Warner sucker
Plants—Willamette daisy, Snake River goldenweed, Applegate milk-vetch, Cook's desert parsley, Malheur wire-lettuce, MacFarlane's four-o'clock

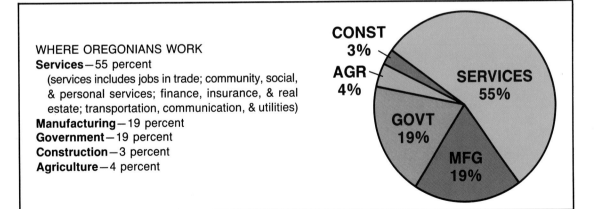

WHERE OREGONIANS WORK
Services—55 percent
  (services includes jobs in trade; community, social, & personal services; finance, insurance, & real estate; transportation, communication, & utilities)
Manufacturing—19 percent
Government—19 percent
Construction—3 percent
Agriculture—4 percent

CONST 3%
AGR 4%
SERVICES 55%
GOVT 19%
MFG 19%

PRONUNCIATION GUIDE

Bonneville (BAHN-uh-vihl)

Cayuse (KEYE-yoos)

Chinook (shuh-NOOK)

Columbia Plateau
   (kuh-LUHM-bee-uh pla-TOH)

Deschutes (dih-SHOOTS)

Eugene (yoo-JEEN)

McLoughlin (muh-KLAWF-luhn)

Nez Percé (NEZ PURS)

Paiute (PEYE-yoot)

Rogue (ROHG)

Umpqua (UHMp-kwaw)

Vancouver (van-KOO-vur)

Willamette (wuh-LAM-uht)

Glossary

archaeologist A person who studies ancient times and peoples by digging up what is left of their cities, buildings, tombs, and other remains.

clear cutting A method of cutting forests that removes all the trees in an area.

canyon A narrow valley that has steep, rocky cliffs on its sides.

desert An area of land that receives only about 10 inches (25 cm) or less of rain or snow a year. Some deserts are mountainous; others are expanses of rock, sand, or salt flats.

hydropower The electricity produced by using water power. Also called hydroelectric power.

immigrant A person who moves into a foreign country and settles there.

irrigation Watering land by directing water through canals, ditches, pipes, or sprinklers.

lava Hot, melted rock that erupts from a volcano or from cracks in the earth's surface and that hardens as it cools.

missionary A person sent out by a religious group to spread its beliefs to other people.

plateau A large, relatively flat area that stands above the surrounding land.

reservation Public land set aside by the government to be used by Native Americans.

treaty An agreement between two or more groups, usually having to do with peace or trade.

Index

The photographs and illustrations in this book are used courtesy of:

Oregon State Parks, pp. 2–3, 12, 14, 54; Department of Environmental Quality, p. 6; Jack Lindstrom, p. 7; Mount Burns, pp. 8–9, 42, 46 (bottom), 49 (right); Emily Slowinski, p. 10; Laura Westlund, pp. 11, 27, 41; Doyen Salsig, p. 13; Jan Gumprecht/Root Resources, p. 15; Larry Schaefer/Root Resources, p. 17; USDA Forest Service, pp. 18, 21, 55, 56, 59 (both), 61; Stan Osolinski/Root Resources, p. 19; Oregon Department of Fish and Wildlife, p. 20; Royal Ontario Museum, Department of Ethnology, Toronto, Canada, p. 22; Oregon Historical Society, pp. 23 (neg. #4466), 25, 29 (neg. # 5231), 30, 35 (neg. #144), 36, 37 (neg. #67701), 39 (neg. #085015), 62 (right, neg. #CN 018349), 63 (lower left & right, negs. #19683 & #26699), 64 (upper & lower left, negs. #251 & #4599), 65 (upper & lower left, negs. #85279 & #78523); University of Minnesota, p. 24; Bryan Peterson/Legislative Media Services, p. 26; Smithsonian Institution National Anthropological Archives, Bureau of American Ethnology Collection, pp. 32 (neg. #2906), 64 (bottom, neg. #43,132); Library of Congress, p. 34; E. Simms/Root Resources, p. 38; Portland Rose Festival Association, pp. 43, 45 (both); Tim Hendrix/Oregon State Fair, p. 44; Hal Denison/Cannon Beach Chamber of Commerce, p. 46 (upper left); Oregon Tourism Division, p. 46 (upper right); Roger & Donna Aitkenhead/Deschutes National Forest, p. 47 (left); Root Resources, pp. 47 (right), 55; © Crystal Images, 1991, Kathleen Marie Menke, pp. 48–49, 52 (left), 68; Deschutes National Forest, p. 50; Rich Iwasaki/Sequent Computers, p. 51; Jan Bannon/Root Resources, pp. 52 (right), 71; Walter Gorham, p. 53; Kenneth W. Fink/Root Resources, p. 61; Minnesota Vikings, p. 62 (middle); New York Public Library, p. 62 (left); Larry Marcus/KCTA TV, p. 63 (upper left); Nike, Inc., p. 63 (upper right); Hollywood Book & Poster Co., p. 64 (upper right); Margaret Miller/William Morrow & Co., p. 65 (upper right); Jean Matheny, p. 66.